Contents

Sport:

Archery

Role:

Guides and leads the girls

Superpower:

Intense sight and spiritual insight

Fear:

Spiders

Special Gadget:

Ancient Compass

Carries:

Bow and Arrow, Ancient Map, Compass

HIDAYAH

JAIDE

Sport:

Skateboarding

Role:

Artist, Racer

Superpower:

Fast racer on foot or skateboard

Fear:

Hunger (She's always hungry!)

Special Gadget:

Time Travel Watch

Carries:

Skateboard, Sketchpad, Pencil, Watch

By Umm Nura

Vancouver

This book is dedicated to all Young Adventurers and Scholars:
Never forget those scholars who have gone before you,
who sacrificed their lives to make your history Golden.
Remember that you come from a line of Great People,
so live your life valiantly as a way to pay your debt.

This book is also dedicated to my little Jannah Jewel, Nura.
Thank you for enveloping me in your light.

Published by Gentle Breeze Books, Vancouver, B.C., Canada

Copyright 2010 by Umm Nura
Illustrations by Nayzak Al-Hilali

Visit us on the Web! www.JannahJewels.com

ISBN: 978-0-9867208-0-2

April 2013

Sport:

Horseback Riding

Role:

Walking Encyclopedia,
Horseback Rider

Superpower:

Communicates with
animals

Fear:

Heights

Special Gadget:

Book of Knowledge

Carries:

Book of Knowledge, has
horse named "Spirit"

Iman

Sara

Sport:

Swimming

Role:

Environmentalist,
Swimmer

Superpower:

Breathes underwater for
a long time

Fear:

Drowning

Special Gadget:

Metal Ball

Carries:

Sunscreen, Water
canteen, Metal Ball

SUPPORTING CHARACTERS

JAFFAR

MANSA MUSA

MASTER ARCHER

THE JANNAH JEWELS ADVENTURE 1:

TIMBUKTU, MALI IN AFRICA

ARTIFACT 1: ANCIENT MANUSCRIPT OF PEACE

"I can only show you the way, but you must make the journey yourself."

~Master Archer to Student

Dear Reader, Assalamu'alaykum,

It is said that the time will come when the peaceful existence of the people of the Earth will be tested and that time has come. The world is in great trouble.

The Jannah Jewels have been called to take on this urgent but dangerous mission. Along the way, they will be tested with burning deserts and tricky thieves, but most importantly they will be tested by their limiting fears. They must learn bravery if they want victory to be theirs.

Come along dear Reader and find out if the Jannah Jewels have what it takes to conquer their fears with courageous faith in the mysterious land of Timbuktu in West Africa.

May peace be with you,
Umm Nura

Prologue

Long ago, there was a famous archer who mastered the way of the Bow and Arrow. He was given the enormous task of protecting the world from evil. He was a peaceful archer, who knew an important secret that made him extremely powerful; not only in archery but also in other ways you would not believe. The secret was written inside a scroll, placed in a box, and locked away inside a giant Golden Clock to be protected from the hands of evil.

But the Master archer was growing old, and the time had come to pass on his duty to an apprentice. He watched his students carefully every day. The students trained extra hard to earn the Master Archer's approval. Two students caught the Master Archer's eye: Khan and Layla. Khan was fierce in his fights, made swift strategies and had strong hands. Layla was flawless in her aim, light on her feet and had intense vision. Khan wanted to be the next master archer more than anything in the world.

Layla, on the other hand, just wanted peace in the world, no matter who became the next Master Archer. Finally, the day dawned when a new Master had to emerge. Despite everyone's surprise and for the first time in history, the duty was given to a girl—Layla. Layla trained relentlessly and over time proved her just and peaceful nature. The Master Archer said, "It is only the humble, the peaceful and those who can control their anger that are allowed to possess the secrets of the bow and arrow."

Before long, Khan and Layla were married and practiced the way of the Bow and Arrow together. In time, they had two children, a boy named Jaffar and a girl named Jasmin.

Jaffar grew up to be a curious and gentle spirit who loved to practice calligraphy, read books, and sit for long hours under shaded trees. Jasmin, on the other hand, liked to play sports, tumble in the grass, and copy her mother in archery. They all lived peacefully together in the old, walled city of Fez in Morocco, *or so it seemed*.

Khan fought with Jaffar, his son, every day, urging him to work harder at archery. Had it been up to Jaffar, he would simply have sat for hours reading his books and practicing calligraphy. He was just not interested in archery, but his father was so fierce that Jaffar had no choice but to practice with his sister, Jasmin, who was a natural. As the days went on, trouble brewed, and gloom and misery settled upon the villa's walls. Over time, Jaffar grew to be an outstanding archer, fierce and powerful, much like his father, despite his not wanting to do so, and soon forgot all about his reading and writing. On the other hand, Layla practiced archery differently. She practiced to refine her skills and herself; she never used archery for fighting, but for strength-building and purifying her heart. Soon, this difference in practicing the Bow and Arrow caused problems for everyone.

*   *   *   *

Far away in Vancouver, Canada, Hidayah was sitting in her classroom, bored as usual. She had always thought that nothing exciting ever happened, but this day everything was about to change. Hidayah was walking home from school when she spotted a mysterious woman in the neighbourhood park. The woman was wearing dark red, flowing robes, and something behind her sparkled in the sunlight. It looked as though she were moving into the empty house on the hill. No one had ever lived there for as long as Hidayah could remember.

Hidayah decided she was done with being bored. So she started the long trek up to the house on the hill. She huffed up the porch stairs and tiptoeing, looked in one of the windows. She couldn't believe what she saw! It was the woman in long, dark red, flowing robes with a bow and arrow in her hands, standing so completely still that she looked like a wax statue. Her strong hands were wrapped around the bow, and her eyes were intently gazing at the target across the room. She was so focused and still that Hidayah had to hold her breath afraid of making any sound. Hidayah sat

mesmerized waiting for the woman to let go of the arrow. *But she did not let go.*

So it happened that day after day, Hidayah would hurry up the hill to watch this mysterious woman. And every day she came closer and closer to the door of the house. Several months went by in this way until one day; Hidayah finally mustered enough courage to sit on the doorstep. Then, for the first time, the woman let go of the arrow, which landed in a perfect spot right in the center of the target. The woman turned and said, "So, you have come." She looked right into Hidayah's eyes as though she was looking through her. Hidayah, at first startled, regained her calmness and with her head lowered said, "My name is Hidayah, may I be your student? Can you teach me the Bow and Arrow?" And the woman replied, "I accepted you as my student the very first day you peeked through the window." Thus, Hidayah trained with the Master Archer for several years and was on her way to becoming a very strong, yet gentle, archer.

1

The Misty Maple Tree

The misty maple tree stood mysteriously in the middle of the neighbourhood park. Four friends sat on the grass near it, tired from playing tag. Hidayah leaned back against the giant trunk. As she closed her eyes, she heard a cracking sound.

"Crunch! Thwump!"

"Hidayah?" asked Iman.

The girls looked right and left, up and down.

"Hidayah?!" She was nowhere to be found. Jaide raced around and around the tree on her skateboard.

"Hidayah, quit playing around, where are you?" said Jaide, pushing against the tree. Suddenly, she heard a similar cracking sound

7

from the tree.

"Crunch! Thwump!"

"Jaide?!"

Jaide was the second to disappear. Astonished, Sara and Iman started pushing the tree.

"Crunch! Thwump!"

The tree trunk opened into a small door. Sara's eyes grew wide with amazement. As the girls peered inside, they saw that the ground beneath them was smooth and curvy. All of a sudden, Iman lost her footing when she leaned over too far. Sara tried to grab Iman back, but it was too late. The girls were sliding down a huge, bark slide and gaining speed.

"Where are weeee?" screamed Sara, holding her hijab in place with one hand.

"We're sliding down into the tree!" exclaimed Jaide. "It was a trap door!"

The maple tree had swept the four girls inside with its twisting, turning slide. They tumbled into a small room.

The girls brushed off twigs and bark dust.

The rough bark walls around them were cold to the touch. It was eerily dark with just a faint light visible.

"Look! Over there," whispered Hidayah. With Hidayah's super eyesight, she was the first to see a glimmer of light near the center of the room. She walked towards it.

"What is that?" whispered Sara. Sara was curious about everything and asked a lot of questions. The girls crept behind Hidayah, huddling one right behind the other. They surrounded an old wooden desk, each girl on one side. There were fascinating objects beckoning in front of them.

"I'm not sure, Sara, but look our names are on these," said Hidayah. "How can that be?"

"It's an ancient compass," whispered Iman, leaning over and peering closely at it. The girls all thought of her as a walking encyclopedia because she always seemed to know everything. "It must be over 100 years old! The compass has your name on it, Hidayah." Iman picked it up.

"Don't touch it!" cried Sara. "Haven't you

read books where touching something makes people fall into more traps, or something comes crashing down?"

"Stop being so paranoid, Sara!" said Iman.

Jaide kicked up her skateboard and propped it against the wall. She started sketching what she saw by the faint light. She loved to draw and never left home without her sketchpad. She chewed on the end of her pencil when she was deep in thought, as she was now. She peered closer.

"This one is yours," said Iman, giving Jaide a large watch. "And this one is mine." Iman brushed dust off a book called, *The Book of Knowledge*, ignoring Sara's pleas.

"SubhanAllah, look at this!" said Iman. "I think it's an ancient map. And, this, this is for Sara."

"What is that?" asked Jaide.

"A metal ball?" said Sara. You girls get all these cool things and I get this metal ball? She turned it around and around in her hand. "Big whoopee!" she sighed.

10

Hidayah and Iman looked closer at the ancient map. But it was hard to see in the flickering light.

"BANG!"

"Uh oh! I knew it!" said Sara. "I told you! You shouldn't have touched that!"

They heard loud clicking footsteps. Jaide started skateboarding around, frantically looking for a way out.

"Ugh, uff." Jaide's skateboard tripped on something in the floor and she went tumbling over. Getting up on her hands and knees, something caught her eye. She brushed away some of the dirt.

"Uh, girls, you might want to come and see this," said Jaide.

"By Allah, it's a gigantic clock! It looks like it's made out of gold! But wait, there are no numbers. There are strange shapes where the numbers for the hours should go," said Iman.

"Look at this. This ancient map has 12 different countries numbered on it and beside each country is some sort of artifact. Wait a minute, each artifact on this map is the same strange shape carved in the Golden Clock!" said Hidayah looking back and forth, from the map to the clock, from the clock to the map.

The footsteps grew even louder.

Suddenly, a woman in dark red, flowing robes entered the room from behind the shadows.

"Sensei Elle!" cried Hidayah. She recognized her immediately.

"Assalamu' alaykum, Hidayah and friends," she said.

"Walaikum asalaam," replied the others looking at each other curiously.

"There is no time to waste. You four have been chosen as the Jannah Jewels. You have a special mission you must complete."

"The Jannah Jewels? I like the sound of that!" said Jaide smiling.

The woman in the dark red robes lit several lanterns hanging along the wall. As the lanterns were lit, it showed several long passages. Her big bow and arrow glistened in the glowing light. The girls sat on their knees around Sensei Elle as she began a story they would never forget.

"Long ago, there was an old Master Archer who had an archery battle to see who would become his apprentice after he was gone. A rough battle ensued between two strong students. In the end, a new Master Archer was chosen. But the loser of the battle felt that he should have won. So, now peace on Earth is being disturbed by this ruthless archer and he has sent his son, Jaffar, to learn the secret of the Bow and Arrow to rule the world. Now, the only way to bring peace back to the world is to find 12 missing artifacts and return them to the Golden Clock before time runs out. It is up to you!"

"What is this Golden Clock?" asked Sara.

"The Golden Clock was created by the old Master Archer, who held the secret of the Bow and Arrow. He wrote this powerful secret on a scroll and locked it into a box. But he felt that the box would not protect the secret well enough. So he decided to make this Golden Clock with instructions on how it works. The Master Archer chose 12 artifacts and carved their exact shapes into the Golden Clock, each at a different hour. Then, he hired a scientist to build a time-travel machine. He used the machine to travel back into time to hide the artifacts in different countries and times, so they cannot be found by just anybody. If all 12 artifacts are found, the secret scroll will be unlocked, and the powerful secret will be unveiled! The old Master Archer believed that there would be a determined and courageous archer, who would be able to find all 12 artifacts, and the powerful secret within the clock was meant for her—to bring harmony back into the world."

"Whoah, whoah, whoah!" exclaimed Jaide. "With all due respect Miss Sensei. There is an evil archer with his son after some mystery scroll and there's a time-travel machine, unlocking some powerful secret? Are we in some movie? Seriously. What does that have to do with us?"

"I think I know!" said Iman.

"Big surprise, we don't call you the walking encyclopedia for nothing!" said Jaide.

"Aren't you listening? If the secret scroll lands in the wrong hands, its powerful secret can be used for great evil," said Iman. "We have been chosen to help!"

"We have been chosen? Why us?" asked Sara.

"Because each of you is training in one of the four elements of archery, horseback riding, swimming, and artistry. You have to work together to defeat Khan, the evil archer," said Sensei Elle.

"What's his problem?" asked Jaide.

"Khan is bitter and angry for losing the battle. He felt that he should have won and been the rightful heir. Now, since only the *young* can travel back into time, he wants to send his only son, Jaffar, to do the deed. Khan can't go himself. You will need to get the artifacts before Jaffar can find them!" explained Sensei Elle.

"Where are the 12 artifacts?" asked Sara.

"I think I know," said Hidayah looking at the ancient map. "It looks like the 12 artifacts are scattered throughout the world."

"Yes, you will travel back into time to recover them. You must return the artifacts here to this Golden Clock. There isn't much time! Jaffar and his father have built their own time-travel machine and know about the artifacts. Jannah Jewels, you must work together to save the world!"

"Where is this time-travel machine and how does it work?" asked Sara.

The Sensei smiled knowingly.

"The tree? *This* maple tree is the time-travel machine!" exclaimed Hidayah.

"All you have to do is close your eyes and say, "BismillahirRahmanirRahim—In the Name of God, Most Merciful, Most Compassionate," with your hearts, and you will end up in the place you have to be to fulfill your mission," said the Sensei.

"But I haven't finished my training," said Hidayah.

"I must go now," said the Sensei. "Hidayah, whenever you ask, you must ask with your heart.

Remember that!" She disappeared as quickly as she had appeared down a long passage. All they could hear were fading footsteps.

"This is crazy. Time-travel tree? Golden Clock? Pinch me, pinch me! I just know it, I'm in a bad dream, wake up Jaide, wake up Jaide."

Sara reached over and pinched Jaide in the shoulder.

"Ow!" screamed Jaide. "Why'd you do that for?"

"We're not in a bad dream! There really is no way out. Snap out of it," said Sara.

Jaide started rolling around on her skateboard. "It's a total dead end!"

"Then there's only one thing to do. We must begin the mission," said Hidayah. "We are always looking for adventure, and now it came looking for us – the Jannah Jewels!"

"Let's go!" said Sara.

"I'm in!" said Iman.

"No way, I'm not going anywhere," said Jaide. "Besides, I'm starving."

"Jaide, quit playing around, you want to

stay down here?" said Hidayah.

At that moment, the last flickering light of a lantern went out.

"No, no, no, don't leave me down here," said Jaide.

"Okay. We say, BismillahirRahmanirRaheem, with our hearts," said Hidayah. "Close your eyes."

They closed their eyes tight, while all four girls said it in unison.

In the blink of an eye they were no longer in the bottom of a maple tree. The Jannah Jewels opened their eyes in an unknown place in an unknown time.

2

Stranded in Sand!

Sand. Everywhere the Jannah Jewels looked, there was just endless sand. They landed right in front of a tree, except that it wasn't a maple tree like back home in Canada. It was a baobab tree. A little farther, as they walked along, they saw wheat growing in neat rows, and animals grazing in nearby fields.

"I can't believe it, we are actually in a completely different country and back in time," said Iman. "How exciting."

"It's blazing hot out here," said Sara. "Here put this on." Sara passed around sunscreen lotion. She was the environmentalist of the four, as she was always finding ways to help the Earth.

"Look at the houses; they are so different from ours back home," said Sara. "It's amazing that whole families can live in these small houses, while back home we live in gigantic houses that only hold three, maybe four, people."

"Our houses back home are more rectangular with pointed roofs," said Jaide sketching away in her drawing book. "These houses are more like small huts, round in shape, that look like they are made out of clay. Look at the thatched roofs."

"There doesn't seem to be anyone around," observed Hidayah. But Hidayah had spoken too soon.

"Salam!"

A small shepherd boy jumped out in front of them, with such dark brown eyes that they almost looked black. He smiled crookedly to one side of his mouth, revealing a big dimple.

"Walaikum asalam!" shouted Iman.

"Ssshh! Not so loud," said Sara. "We don't want to draw attention to ourselves."

"He seems harmless, lighten up Sara," said Iman.

Behind him the girls saw about a dozen camels and twice as many lambs grazing. His curious, dark brown eyes were staring at the objects in their hands. The Jannah Jewels quickly placed their things out of view. Iman spotted the horses in the open fields. She had a horse named Spirit back home. She loved animals and had a way of communicating with them.

"This is my favorite tree," said the shepherd boy, sitting down next to it. "I rest under it every day when the sun reaches its zenith. I've never seen you before. Are you visiting on a caravan route with the King?"

"We are sort of lost, we, uh, kind of strayed far away from home, where exactly are we?" asked Jaide stammering in her broken Arabic.

"You are never lost. Allah always knows where you are, so you are never really lost to begin with," said the shepherd boy with his crooked smile. "You are very near to Timbuktu's

Great Mosque."

"Timbuktu! It's a real place? I've always thought of it as some mysterious land, an unreachable legend. I can't believe it actually exists. We're actually in Timbuktu!" said Sara excitedly.

The boy looked strangely at Sara. Jaide gave Sara her stern eye to be quiet. The boy remained sitting by the tree as the sun stayed at its peak for a few minutes and then slowly dipped down.

"Ah, you might want to look after that camel over there, he's pretty far from the rest of the group," said Hidayah, using her super eyesight.

The boy jumped to his feet looking really worried.

"Oh, thanks!" said the shepherd boy. "I would be in a lot of trouble if I lost a camel or a lamb. These animals are my family's only hope for survival in the desert, but things will be changing soon when the King arrives."

"Who is this King he keeps talking about?"

asked Sara. "He seems so excited by him."

"I have a feeling we are going to find out," said Hidayah.

The shepherd boy circled up his animals and walked them into a wooden, gated area. Then, he ran down a long, straight path toward a very large mud building.

"C'mon, you're going to be late!" said the boy.

"Late for what?" asked Jaide. "I hope it's lunch; I'm hungry!"

"Stop thinking about your stomach!" said Sara. "We're on an important mission, and all you can think about is food."

"My mom had dinner almost ready. Homemade pizza!" said Jaide. "It's not my fault my stomach has a monster in it. I didn't know we would be swallowed up by some crazy tree and whisked away like we are on some flying carpet. Things like this don't happen every day, you know."

"So what are we supposed to do now?" asked Sara.

"Let's follow the boy, maybe he can help us," said Hidayah.

They walked past many shops, all lined up together. There were stalls of cotton cloth in all the colors of the rainbow. The girls watched as a woman skillfully took out fresh loaves of bread on a flat pan and displayed them in a pyramid shape. Many people were bargaining with the shop-keepers. They paid for their purchases with what looked like gold nuggets and shells you would find on the beach. Other people traded cloth for bread, or handmade jewellery for rice.

As the Jannah Jewels approached, they saw a large crowd of people gathered around the huge mud building listening to a speech by someone.

"Oh, wow! This is the Jingereber Mosque! It was built entirely from mud in the year 1325," said Iman, flipping through *The Book of Knowledge* she got from the tree.

"A Gingerbread house?" asked Jaide.

"No! Not Gingerbread, Jingereber!" said

Iman. Her voice indicated she was clearly annoyed.

"Thank you for gathering today for the grand opening of the Jingereber Mosque," said a tall man with blue robes and a blue turban.

"Grand opening?" asked Jaide.

"We must be in the 14th Century!" said Hidayah.

Everyone was wearing long, traditional, flowing robes in bright colors, and many men were wearing matching turbans. Women and young girls were wearing the hijab; some wore them in the style of a turban, while others wore them like shawls wrapped snugly around them. Some of the women had babies tied to their backs in long pieces of cloth.

Jaide opened up her sketchbook and drew a picture of the mud mosque. She wanted to remember it, *if she ever got back home*.

"That's so environmentally friendly to use natural resources to make the building," said Sara. "Too bad people back home can't be more resourceful."

"Look what I found," said Iman. "It says here that the Quranic Sankore University, had almost 50,000 students at one point. It was built by Al-Sahili. He was from the Spanish city of Granada. It says here in *The Book of Knowledge* that Al-Sahili was asked to build it by the Golden King."

"The *Golden* King? That must be the king the shepherd boy was talking about," said Hidayah making a connection.

"Let's take a closer look at the mosque," said Iman. "I bet we can see some of the famous manuscripts."

"Manuscripts?" asked Jaide, looking around worriedly. "I don't know about this—we have got to be careful."

But it was too late. Iman was already running up to the crowd to get a closer look.

3

The Stolen Manuscript

"It says here that there are probably around 650,000 manuscripts and counting in the city!" said Iman.

Squeezing past people right and left through the crowd, the girls finally reached the mosque. Hidayah's eyes widened when she saw it. She loved architecture and fine details in things. Her bow and arrow was also a famous, ancient piece. It had belonged to a Master Archer back in the 8th century and had been handed down in her family for generations. There was a beautiful inscription on the bow in Arabic. It was from a hadith, a traditional saying, from the Prophet Muhammad, peace and blessings be upon him. The Prophet Muhammad had this written on the hilt of his sword, it read, "Forgive him who wrongs you; join him who cuts you off; do good to him who does evil to you, and speak the truth although it be against yourself."

The mosque in front of her was different from any she had ever seen. The walls were made of the earth itself. It was simple, yet elegant. Her fingers grasped the ancient compass she had kept in her pocket from the tree; it felt cool and smooth to the touch.

Jaide put her pencil and notebook into her backpack and ran to catch up to the others.

As they got closer to the entrance, they blended into the crowd of people all waiting to have a look inside the new mosque. Suddenly, loud shouting was heard from within the crowd. A small circle opened around a man who was talking about someone special who would be arriving at any minute.

"So, Encyclopedia Iman, just who are they expecting?" asked Sara.

"Ssshh, let me listen. Ah, yes. I should've known. The Golden King is none other than

Mansa Musa. Hidayah, you were right. He was known as the Golden King because he brought many riches to this part of the world. He brought so much gold that Mali was recognized on the world map as a thriving country."

"Listen, there seems to be a problem over there," said Sara on her tiptoes.

The Jannah Jewels moved closer. Hidayah tried to hide her bow and arrow as much as she could.

The girls moved up just in time to see the little shepherd boy standing alone by the door of the Jingereber Mosque. He was anxiously staring at the girls. His brown eyes were darting back and forth. His dimpled smile was no more.

"He's up to something. Let's follow him!" said Iman.

"Wait a minute, it looks like he is being chased," said Hidayah. "Look!"

A man with black robes and a black turban slipped inside the mosque after him. Most of the crowd was still listening to the speech announcing the Golden King. The black-robed man had piercing, iron-grey eyes. A sharp, curved knife on his belt glimmered in the sun. Hidayah felt a shiver down her spine. There was something lurking behind those eyes.

After a few seconds, they heard a bellowing scream followed by bleating sheep and neighing horses. The animals scurried all about.

"My manuscript, it's gone! Someone stole my manuscript!"

"That doesn't sound too good," said Sara.

"And there's no time for lunch," said Jaide.

Hidayah rolled open the ancient map. She searched it until she found a small symbol of what looked like a scroll on the continent of Africa. Beside the tiny scroll were these words:

Timbuktu, Mali
Artifact: Manuscript

"The stolen manuscript is the first artifact that we need to find," said Hidayah, rolling the map back up.

"What are we waiting for? Let's go!" said Sara. "It's time to complete this mission."

4

The Chase

The girls slid past the crowd as people poured inside to get a glimpse of the Great Mosque.

"Why would someone want to steal manuscripts?" whispered Jaide.

"These manuscripts are very important. They reveal that Africa was truly a literate continent, and it would rewrite history as we know it," said Iman.

"What does that mean, to rewrite history?" asked Jaide.

"It means that whatever we know of history is through certain people and their memory; we don't know how much of it is exactly true. People back home don't realize how much the Islamic civilization actually led the world in chemistry, astronomy, physics, optics, and more," said Iman looking at her *Book of Knowledge*. "These manuscripts would reveal that."

"Sshh, look over there—it's a *griot*. He is an elder, a storyteller who passes down stories to the younger ones. That's one way of preserving history," whispered Hidayah. "Then the younger ones will pass it on, and so it will go."

"Yes, exactly. I was just reading here that a man named Ibn Battuta travelled for almost 23 years, and he came to Mali, too. He was known as a world traveler and wrote a book called the *Rihla*. It is a valuable eyewitness account of history that we can trust to tell us about what happened in Mali."

"But if we are back in time, Ibn Battuta hasn't written the book yet," said Sara. "I'll read it when I get back home."

"*If* we ever get back home," said Jaide.

"Would you stop saying that!" said Iman.

"Ibn Battuta must have travelled by horse, donkey cart, or camel," said Sara. "It's a lot better for the environment than using cars and airplanes."

"The boy, he's over there!" said Hidayah.

The shepherd boy was exiting through another door in the mosque. The girls ran to catch up. He was already far into the desert on the other side. He covered up the back of a camel with a large blanket. Then he quickly tapped the camel on its back, and the camel was led away by another shepherd.

Sara took out sunscreen and passed it around to all the girls. "Here, put this on. The UV-rays out here are pretty dangerous."

The girls followed the shepherd boy through the hot desert at a safe distance. Everything was eerily quiet and still in the desert than the commotion at the Great Mosque. The sun was slowly bowing down behind the tops of the sand dunes.

"We have to keep following him. He might know something about the manuscript," said Iman.

"Or he might *have* the manuscript!" said Jaide.

"Ssshhh, okay, stay close. We don't want to lose him," said Hidayah.

The girls came to a small clearing with many mud huts. The boy had completely disappeared. Could he be in one of the mud huts? But all of the mud huts looked exactly the same!

"These mud huts..." said Iman. "Sometimes the people would hide their manuscripts inside their homes."

The girls all walked around looking for the young boy. Even though the sun was almost at the horizon, it was still very hot. The boy was nowhere to be seen.

"He knows we're following him, and he's hiding," said Sara wiping sweat off her eyebrow.

"He's probably having some amazing African lunch, while we bake out here in the desert sand like eggs in a frying pan," said Jaide. "Sunny side up eggs, that is."

They sat exhausted behind a sand dune. Hidayah took out her compass and began fiddling with the gadget. She sat mesmerized by it. "I wish I knew where the boy was, and what he is up to."

Whenever you ask, you must ask with your heart. Hidayah remembered the Sensei's advice. She closed her eyes tighter and tried again.

"Bismillah. Please, Allah, the Most Generous, you've helped me before in so many situations. Please help me again. I wish I knew where the boy was, and what he is up to!"

All of a sudden, Hidayah stood up. She had a strong feeling in her heart that knew where to go. She looked at the compass and walked in one direction for a short while. She walked until she reached a large sand dune in the middle of a remote part of the desert. The girls followed close behind.

"There's the camel and the boy!" exclaimed Jaide. "What are they doing?"

"Alhamdulillahi Rabbil Alameen. Thank you Allah!" Hidayah said.

"Faster, faster, before he finds us. Dig!" said a tall man with blue robes and a blue turban. The shepherd boy was by his side.

The girls crept behind the sand dune.

"Looks like they're burying—"

"Ooooeew," screamed Sara. Jaide ran over and put her hand over Sara's mouth, muffling her scream.

Something glided across the desert and landed right behind the sand dune where the girls were hiding.

5

Buried Treasure

Hidayah instinctively pulled out her bow and arrow and the girls all took up their fighting stance.

"Wait, wait!" yelled Iman.

It was the man with the iron-grey eyes. He quickly moved past them and went towards the shepherd boy and the man.

"Quick, we have to create a distraction," said Iman.

The girls started jumping up and down to startle the lambs and sheep, which then scurried all about. Suddenly, the man with the iron-grey eyes was trapped in the middle. The Jannah Jewels watched as he twisted and turned and finally made his way through the animals. The man with the iron-grey eyes wiped sweat off his face and tried to catch his breath. He held up his fist in anger at the Jannah Jewels as he stumbled and tripped his way across the sand.

"Jaide, check your time-travel watch from the tree, how much time do we have left?" asked Hidayah.

"55 minutes!" said Jaide.

"Remember what the Sensei said that we can't stay in the past for a long time and if we don't solve the mystery before time runs out, we'll be stuck here and it will change the past forever."

The girls ran up to join the shepherd boy and the man, and all of them quickly ran away into another part of the desert to escape the man with the iron-grey eyes in case he decided to come back.

"These manuscripts must be pretty special," said Sara.

"The knowledge in these manuscripts is worth more than any other thing here, even food," said the shepherd boy. "The villagers here in Timbuktu understand the wealth in these manuscripts. They are hiding them away from people who want to change what it says in history."

"Why would people want to change the history?" asked Sara. "That doesn't seem right."

"Because the manuscripts will show the world Africa's great power as a continent that flourished in science, math, law, medicine, religion and more. Some people just don't appreciate or understand the people here in Timbuktu and all they have done for civilization," said the man with the boy. "Yet others will just try to sell the manuscript for money not understanding their real value."

"Let's go! We have to get going and complete this mission," said Hidayah.

"Or we might be stuck here forever!" said Jaide.

"It wouldn't be so bad to be stuck in one of the most exciting Islamic times ever," said Iman.

"Oh, c'mon, Iman, your family will miss you. We have to go back home!" said Sara.

The girls watched the shepherd boy and the man in the blue robes dig another hole in the desert. They kept looking around to see if anyone was watching. Then they opened up a big case and put something inside of it. Many cases seemed to be hidden underground. They began covering up the case with sand.

"These people, they have to protect their writings and the knowledge contained in them," said Hidayah.

"Jaide, how much more time do we have now to solve the mystery?" asked Iman.

Jaide looked at the time-travel watch again. "40 minutes!"

Hidayah put away her bow and arrow and took out her special compass. She sat down exhausted from the heat of the desert.

Sara passed around her water canteen. "Drink up," she said. "The heat can dry out even the deepest oasis."

"Allah helped me just a second ago. He

will surely help me again," said Hidayah. "Bismillah. Ya Allah, please help us to find the stolen manuscript and solve the mystery."

At first nothing happened.

"Try again. Really mean it. Hidayah, use your heart," said Iman.

"Bismillah. Please, Allah, you always help me in every situation. I know you will help us again. Help us to find the stolen manuscript and solve the mystery!"

At last, Hidayah got another feeling, and she opened up her eyes. "This way!" called Hidayah. The girls slapped hands and ran after her in the direction of another large building. It was one of the many madrasahs or Quranic schools in Timbuktu.

"Watch out!" called Iman.

As Hidayah turned, she slammed right into someone. It wasn't the little boy. It wasn't the man with the blue robes. It was a very large man in beautiful robes with a giant staff made out of shining gold in his right hand. He seemed to be shimmering like the golden rays of the morning sun. People around him were carrying gifts of pure gold and platters of various treasures.

All four girls stared at him wide-eyed and open-mouthed.

"Who, who," stammered Jaide. "Who are *you*?"

6

The Golden King

"You're—you're Mansa Musa! You are one of the greatest kings! You have one of the widest kingdoms and the largest armies. I have heard about how brave you were over your enemies, and how you have given people many gifts!" exclaimed Iman. She really was a walking encyclopedia.

The man chuckled and began to speak in Arabic.

"I am Mansa Musa," he said. "I am King of Mali. You must be the Jannah Jewels. You have come from the future to help find the ancient manuscript and restore balance to the Earth, correct?"

"Yes, we have!" said Sara.

"I have believed in Africa for a long time. I believe in its history and its academic and spiritual power. You have to go back home and tell the world what it was like here in Timbuktu."

"But won't people just come and steal the books and use them for their own purposes?" asked Iman.

"Yes, some will. But the knowledge buried in these books needs to be known to the wide world. There is a lot of inaccurate history out there. Stories only told from one point of view, one kind of people, one nation, one tribe. It's time we tell our story, too."

"We can do it!" said Jaide, jumping onto her skateboard.

"You must find the ancient manuscript and restore the balance," said the King.

"This particular manuscript is really important, isn't it?" asked Hidayah.

"It has a cure for many diseases and also laws that will help unite people. The laws in these manuscripts will teach people how to live together in peace."

"They are manuscripts of peace!" said Hidayah.

"Yes. Thieves are already after these manuscripts because they can sell them for a lot of money. But the villagers want to keep them safe because their father, or grandfather, or great-grandfather, or great-great grandfather wrote them."

"We will help you!" said Hidayah.

Just then, Hidayah had a feeling so strong in her heart that she thought it was going to burst. "It's this way girls. I can feel it," she said. "Let's go!"

The girls raced behind Hidayah.

7

Mistaken Identity

The reddish sun filled the sky with orange, pink, red, and purple. It looked like a painter's palette. Hidayah pulled the compass out of her bag. Jaide opened up her sketchbook and bit the end of her pencil. She sketched Hidayah's compass in her book.

"Are you all right?" asked Jaide, gasping for air after their run.

"Yeah. I was thinking about Jaffar. You know, I've heard he is a very strong archer."

"But you trained long and hard with the Sensei," said Jaide.

"My training hasn't gone so well in the last few months. I'm a little worried," said Hidayah.

"Don't worry, we will all be there to help

if the time comes that you have to face him. But, inshaAllah, God willing, you won't have to, because we will beat him in finding the artifacts, and balance will be restored to the Earth once again."

"Thanks," said Hidayah, and she leaned over and hugged Jaide.

"All right, all right, none of this mushy stuff," said Jaide.

They entered the madrasah through doors made of Earth. The smell of fresh paper, ink, and dust filled the air. There were hundreds of people everywhere. There were judges, priests, and teachers pouring over handwritten manuscripts and sitting in small circles. Mansa Musa had brought back many people of knowledge when he returned from his pilgrimage to Mecca. The school was humming with voices. The Jannah Jewels heard conversations of all kinds.

"The Niger River is the region's main waterway and helps Timbuktu as a trading city. We need to use it to get to Taghaza, where the salt mines are located," said a scholar with a white turban. "We need a lot of salt to make our medicine."

In the corner of the madrasah, the Jannah Jewels saw young children studying the Holy Quran on wooden tablets. Some were writing verses from the Quran on it with black ink; some were reciting from the board; and some were memorizing it with a teacher.

Hidayah walked around observing everything. Was the thief in here? How would they find him in here with so many people? Why did I have the feeling to come here? thought Hidayah.

She continued farther into the school. They entered a small room.

The Jannah Jewels walked in and couldn't believe their eyes. Thousands of loose pages, manuscripts, and books were on the shelves, on the tables, on the chairs, everywhere!

Jaide checked her watch. "29 minutes!"

"Ssshhh. Look over there, what's happening?" asked Sara.

The girls hid behind the bookshelves.

The man in the blue robes was backed up against the wall. His feet dangled a foot off the floor, while a man with black robes grilled him with questions.

"Hand it over! Give me the manuscript!"

"Hey, let him go!" said Hidayah. She reached for her bow and arrow.

She quickly put an arrow into the bow and shot at the man with the black robes. She had perfect aim. She caught one end of his shirt, and he landed against the wall. She quickly got another arrow and caught the other end of his shirt. There he was hanging off the mud walls by two big arrows. He wriggled back and forth trying to get loose.

"Thank you for saving my life!" said the man in the blue robes, and he ran off through the library chuckling. Something in his voice sounded eerily familiar.

Iman walked up to the thief and looked inside the pocket. No manuscript. She looked inside the other one, no manuscript.

"Give us the manuscript!" said Iman.

"I don't have it!" he said.

"Baba? Hey, let my father down from there!"

It was the little shepherd boy.

"You've got the wrong person!" he said.

"What? It couldn't be!" said Iman.

"I'm the boy's father! Look underneath my hood," said the man.

Iman's hands were quivering too much. Jaide rolled by on her skateboard and flipped over the black hood of the black robes.

The girls gasped at what they saw! It was the father of the boy.

"The thief switched the robes!"

8

The Hooded Thief

"Time is running out!" said Sara.

"12 minutes left to be exact!" said Jaide. "And, we're running out of clues."

Just then, the little shepherd boy burst in breathlessly.

"Come quickly!"

They followed the little boy through a wooden door and a long hallway. They came to an even larger mud door with a tiny latch. Sara pushed it open. It opened with a loud bang. It led to a stable.

There they saw a camel standing by itself with a big blue blanket over its humps. Iman held out her hand to the camel's nose. She began to talk to it and rub its face. Iman had

grown up with animals her entire life. She had a gift of understanding what animals were trying to say.

After a few minutes had passed, Iman lifted up the blanket. There were hundreds of manuscripts bundled up, hidden under the blanket.

Camels were very important in Mali and in other countries that wanted to trade goods in desert areas. Camels were known for being able to go without food or water for a couple of days. They could carry up to 400 pounds and travel more than 15 miles a day. Camels were the reason why trade routes opened up for West Africa and the rest of the world. They are truly amazing animals, and that is why they are also mentioned in the Holy Quran.

"The thief is hiding these manuscripts on this camel, and he's pretending to be one of the locals!"

"Did you hear that? Someone's coming! Hide!" said Sara.

The girls hid behind different boxes

scattered in the stable. Then a man with blue robes entered with loud steps, the door banging behind him. He walked over to the camel and reached for the blanket. The camel backed away, bumping into boxes, sensing danger.

"I've finally got the famous manuscript!" cried the thief. "Now, to find the Golden Clock."

Again the voice sounded eerie to Hidayah.

"Oh, no, you don't! You're not getting away this time!" said Hidayah.

She took her bow and arrow and tied a piece of rope to the end of it. She shot the arrow up through the roof. Jaide quickly jumped on her skateboard and grabbed the rope, rolling it around and around the thief, tying him up. Sara reached into his bag and found the ancient manuscript. She held it in her hand. The manuscript felt so wonderful to touch.

"Who are you, and why are you after this manuscript?" asked Iman.

Iman repeated herself. But she was met with silence.

Hidayah nervously flipped back the man's

hood with one end of the arrow. The iron-grey eyes pierced into hers.

"You! You're Jaffar!"

The two opponents glared at each other. Jaffar's eyes were streaked red with anger as he wrestled back and forth in the tightly wound rope.

"It's not over, Hidayah. I will fulfill this mission for my father!" shouted Jaffar. He kept wriggling back and forth, but then his eyes fell upon the ancient compass in Hidayah's hand.

"That compass, where did you get that?" said Jaffar.

Hidayah moved it out of his reach just as he lurched forward for it. He fell to the ground. Dust filled the air as the girls coughed.

"You will be sorry of the day you crossed me!" said Jaffar.

Hidayah's hands were wet with sweat and the vein in her temple was throbbing like a heartbeat after a long race. "Not this time, Jaffar."

They all entered the star-filled night,

victorious.

"Mansa Musa! We did it! We found the ancient manuscript!"

"Mansa Musa, Sir?"

He was nowhere to be found.

"Maybe, he was just a mirage?" said Sara. "You know, it's when you see things in the desert, but they are not really real, only they sort of seem real. It usually happens when you are close to dehydration." Sara drank from her bottle, but only a few drops were left.

"No way, it couldn't be, we all saw that shimmering gold and we talked to him!" said Jaide.

But they still couldn't find him. Instead they found the shepherd boy and his father and handed them the camel with the manuscripts. Hidayah tucked the special manuscript, the artifact for the Golden Clock, into her jacket. The villagers gathered around and raised the Jannah Jewels in the air in celebration.

"1 minute!" cried Jaide.

9

Trapped in the Trunk

Iman took out a map of Timbuktu that told them how to get back home, but she couldn't quite read the Maghribi script it was written in. The shepherd boy walked over and took the map. Finally his face lit up, and his perfect white teeth gleamed in the sunlight.

"Go straight down this road, and go right. The tree you are looking for is there."

The shepherd boy gave his 'salam' with his crooked smile and waved. Iman whistled for a horse and grabbed Hidayah. Sara hopped on behind Jaide on her skateboard. The girls flew at lightning speed as their hijabs fluttered in the wind.

Finally, they made it. Hidayah pushed

against the tree, but it wouldn't move.

"All together, girls, c'mon!"

The girls pushed with all their might. They heard a familiar clickity-clack, and the tree trunk opened up and swallowed up the girls. Down, down, down they went and landed with a big thwump!

Hidayah landed first, crashing into the desk; then Jaide, Sara and Iman all bumped right into Hidayah, one right after the other.

"Uphf, ugh, ow, eek."

"We made it!"

"Ah, not quite, we're still trapped in the tree!"

10

Painted Wall of Secrets

"How do we get out of here? The Sensei told us to come back before time ran out," said Sara. "We made it before time ran out, right?"

Jaide looked anxiously at her watch. It read 0:03. Then, Hidayah saw a house shape on the map. It said "Canada" beside it.

"I think I know girls," said Hidayah. "C'mon! Say BismillahirRahmanirRaheem!" The Jannah Jewels closed their eyes.

In the blink of an eye, they opened their eyes to an *almost* familiar place in an *almost* familiar time.

The girls looked around and couldn't see anything. Sara bent down and found two sticks. She gathered some leaves and twigs and rubbed the sticks together. She made a small fire. Then, she carried a burning stick to light up some of the lanterns hanging from the walls. The flickering light bounced on the walls around them. The walls revealed a picture of an archery battle.

"Who are they?" said Iman, wide-eyed.

Hidayah peered closely at a woman with a bow and arrow poised in the painting.

"You mean you actually don't know something?" said Sara.

Iman playfully punched Sara in the shoulder.

"This is a legend from long ago," said the Sensei.

The girls looked behind them. It was Sensei Elle. Hidayah held up the first artifact to show her.

"You found the first piece of the puzzle, you should be proud of yourselves."

Hidayah took the artifact and walked over to the Golden Clock. She bent down and put the artifact at the hour of one o' clock. It fit exactly, and when it was in place, it lit up, glowing like the morning sun.

"1-down, 11 more to go."

Hidayah peered at the picture on the wall more closely. There was something about that woman. But, she couldn't quite see her face. And who was that pointing the arrow towards her?

"You will need to remember the words of the wise before you, so you can help restore balance on Earth. It's up to you now, Jannah Jewels."

The girls all looked at one another and gulped.

11

Homebound

It was finally time for the Jannah Jewels to go home.

"Did you see how that Golden Clock lit up?" asked Sara. "It was amazing!"

"We have to train hard to find the artifacts. Jaffar was too close already," said Hidayah. "Not only am I training in archery; but, Sara, you must master swimming; Jaide, you must master art; and, Iman, you must master horseback riding. We have to work together."

Iman took the map from Hidayah and unrolled it. "There are a lot of artifacts on here. That means a lot more adventures for the Jannah Jewels."

Jaide rolled by on her skateboard. "But,

right now, it's time for some dinner."

"Jaaaide!" groaned the girls.

"What? A growing girl has got to eat!" she said. "Anybody for homemade pizza?"

The girls followed Jaide to her house for dinner with their arms entwined over one another's shoulders.

Do the Jannah Jewels have what it takes to beat Jaffar? Will the girls find the next missing artifact for the Golden Clock? Will they find it before time runs out?

Find out in the next adventure, the *Chase in China* for more clues to the mystery of the Golden Clock.

Don't miss the next Jannah Jewels book!

In the second book, the girls are caught and thrown aboard the ship of Zheng He, the famous Chinese Muslim Admiral. Caught in a lightning thunderstorm, they must sail in raging waters to retrieve a rare artifact. Can the Jannah Jewels escape the fiery arrows of pirates and make it safely back home?

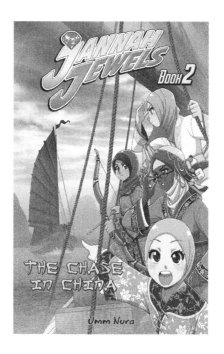

Find out more about the second book by visiting our website at www.JannahJewels.com

Glossary

Alhamdulillahi Rabbil Alameen: "All praise is due to God" in Arabic. This prayer is said when thankful of something or to show appreciation.

Allah: God

Assalamu'alaykum: "May the peace of God be with you" in Arabic.

BismillahirRahmanirRaheem: "In the name of God, Most Merciful, Most Beneficient" in Arabic. This prayer is said before partaking in something.

Hijab: a head-scarf

InshaAllah: "If it is God's will" in Arabic. It is said when indicating hope for something to occur in the future.

Jannah: heaven, paradise or garden

Madrasah: a school

Maghribi script: It is one of the cursive forms

of the Arabic alphabet that developed in North Africa and later in Andalusia.

Mosque: A sacred place of worship for Muslims, also commonly called a masjid.

Quran: The last holy scripture of the Muslims.

Rihla: The title of Ibn Battuta's travel account, also means, a 'journey' in Arabic.

SubhanAllah: "Glory be to God" in Arabic. This prayer is said when in awe of something.

Walaikum asalaam: "May the peace of God be upon you too" in Arabic

IMAN

To find out more about our other books,

go to:

www.JannahJewels.com

.

Lightning Source UK Ltd.
Milton Keynes UK
UKOW06f2129030116

265644UK00006B/88/P